# Bukchon

## Poems of Shin Dal-Ja

# Bukchon

## Poems of Shin Dal-Ja

Translated by Cho Young-Shil

Homa & Sekey Books
Paramus, New Jersey

Library of Congress Cataloging-in-Publication Data
Bukchon / : poems of Shin Dal-Ja ; translated by Cho
Young-Shil.
ISBN 9781622461134 (paperback)
LC classification PL992.73.T34 P8513 2023
https://lccn.loc.gov/2023008953

Published by Homa & Sekey Books
3rd Floor, North Tower
Mack-Cali Center III
140 E. Ridgewood Ave.
Paramus, NJ 07652

Tel: 201-261-8810, 800-870-HOMA
Fax: 201-261-8890
Email: info@homabooks.com
Website: www.homabooks.com

Printed in the USA
1 3 5 7 9 10 8 6 4 2

# TABLE OF CONTENTS

# Author's Note

Unpacking my furniture and belongings in Gyedong, I thought the house and I both are in the hands of fate. Never once did I imagine this. That I was to live in Bukchon,* Jongrogu, and to live in a small ten-pyung* house with one room to sleep in, barely stretching my legs…. Lighting a hanji-covered* lamp after having arranged a minimal number of items, tossing about unable to slide into sleep the first night, I had a vague notion I would make a poetry book entitled *Bukchon*.

That is what happened the first night after moving in, so I opened a new notebook and wrote down "Bukchon". It was merely a flashing thought to begin with, but as I looked closely and from afar into Gyedong's alleys, into Gawhoedong's pine path and Bukchon's cultural tradition, my thought was consolidated.

When you get used to everything, your thoughts inevitably grow dull. So too, once accustomed to the environment, the amazement and sensitivity will diminish.

That is why I committed myself to setting about writing while the sensitivity and wonder was intact, before the familiarity with things cloaked a pall over the mind.

---

*Bukchon is transliteration of North Village.
*10 pyungs will be approximately 356 square feet.
*Hanji is traditional Korean paper.

A brief time in Bukchon brought me new experiences and amazement, and it was a joy to translate a part of Seoul, which was my dwelling place, into my life and my living. There were too many stories of Bukchon I did not know of, though living in Seoul. There was nothing in the history, in the full tradition, that did not captivate me.

Of course Bukchon exhibited conflict with changes. Bukchon, however, evidently was a real sweet place, and the people there were also such that I wanted to love.

While I lived in Bukchon I was ill all along. And my desire was shaken to its root by throbbing pains from a chronic illness, which I bore up with dutiful desire for the writing of *Bukchon*.

This poetry book might be a mere depiction of some finger of Bukchon.

Although I have neither seen nor written of the entire Bukchon, I summoned the courage to publish this poetry book, considering this a virtual little smile for the love of Bukchon. And hang at the beginning of the book this little poem like a doorknob.

Ten-pyung hanok it is
Feet touching, head touching,
a room the size of a garden balsam seed
To have company with the afternoon sunlight
warming my hands over the sunlight seeping through hanji
Like the bosom of my home
like the bosom of my mother
when I was little, living in a hanok
No
Like a homecoming in old age

# Part I

# A House Facing North

South on my back

my eyes ascend Samcheong Park;

the first light

streams through my hanji-lined window

I see the rising sunlight, perhaps sensing my earnest,

coming round and round

swiftly to alight

on the incisor-sized garden of my north-facing house

I see the cerulean early light

turning ruddy as gum

## Coolness

You do not need a large wall for putting up an address

You do not need a big garden for setting up one stick

Why need a large room for making up one's mind

While defrosting a bowl of frozen rice

a day the size of a grain of rice goes by

# Tree Fragrance of Hanok*

Felled with an axe
cut in pieces
severed from the root
scattered
planed by a carpenter
smoothed
at last to be erected pillar of the house
and nailed here and there
yet when I enter the house
ah what a pure tree fragrance....

---

*Hanok is transliteration of traditional Korean house.

## Autumn in Gyedong

In a Syberian chrysanthemum

leaf of a room

I lie

shielding against 52 degrees chill

with a comforter the size of a petal

and think of the one solitary petal

of tomorrow

then tremble

alone

# Footprints of Light

The one that steals into the wall of my room as afternoon
    comes on

Through south-facing window, the sun's shadow in cross
    stripes

enters the room;

where did I see that pattern, I wonder

So very friendly figure, who was it

Is that a face, or a scenery that brushed past my life

That figure, that warmth, drawing my blood,

I want to show into a place more affable than my body

# Red Water

Today
I dipped both my hands in a washbasin
and see the water turning red
Maybe the thing that seeps out of my ten fingernails
are the dreams
injured while tossing about in my body

Maybe the heart's excessive poison
suffered
unable even to move on

Maybe the blood flowing where I changed my mind
as I pressed on my way all night
then, as overturning the earth, whirled about

This water
I say I have nowhere to throw out

# The Moon of Gyedong

Was there ever a road companion like this
As I ambled to Gyedong alley
from the National Museum of Modern Art
a truly ancient voice came to me
The moon furtively taking my arm in his
tells me that we take this night to the end of the earth
Yes, let's!
I wanted to live wildly as that
Wanted to live at least once without rhyme and reason,
     without reckoning loss and gain

I am alight with a single-minded will
but where has the moon gone away

## Bogus Shoes

On the stepstone of a hanok where a single woman lives
lie clumsily men's shoes

Signifying I do not live by myself,
no way,
I've gotten from villagers
men's sneakers and shoes
and today big army shoes to intimidate a bit
and placed in the middle of the stepstone

Who is he with no body but shoes
A formless eeriness
Others have no doubts nor fear
but I am more terrified opening the door in the morning,
Who's that?
Waves of loneliness washing over still more chilling,
a pair of bogus shoes

# Late Night

Two o'clock at night
when I open my eyes and switch on the light
alone
As I open a window of my hanok I see
another window lit far away

Who lives inside that window?

I wonder if my window will also be beautiful
when looked on from farther up
If I too will be a longing afar
like an astral flower barely in bloom

Two o'clock at night
A time for a genial way to open
to meet anybody when you hold out your hand anywhere

I curl up into a ball
and try to roll

## My Village Bukchon

I thought ten p'yong only was mine
but the whole Bukchon is mine

Gyedong, Wonseodong, Gawhoedong, Samcheongdong,
Jeongdok Public Library, the Constitutional Court, the
    Board of Audit & Inspection,
the National Museum of Art, Samcheong Park, Changdeok
    Palace, Folklore Museum,
everywhere I walk, unquestionably these are all mine

Tradition and culture interpenetrate to a flow
The street where time binds pierced pains to a restoration
When tradition fosters and culture supports
the road broadening with alleyways, closing then opening
    their eyes

Today
alley after alley whispering, on every stairway sunlight
    shining
Foreigners passing by the alley
take photos of my house the size of a cherry

All of Bukchon is yours

# Gongildang*

Bukchon-ro 8-gil 26
Above the gate of my hanok just the size of a business card
hangs the house name Gongildang
It is the name Rev. Musan Seorak
embroidered pretty as flowers
with a waft of wind captured, a sea of Seorak roundly
    imprinted
A word from Mrs. Kim Namjo:
The letter Gong (empty) for a single woman's house is
    rather....
All emptied out, then it is to be piled up anew
Empty to be ten thousand
Single or double or emptied out or piled up
all the same
At that moment time rolls to a halt, then goes on
Single doubles up, and double is becoming one
Sunday, a day to be filled with worship

---

*Gongildang is the transliteration of the Sunday House.

13

## Sleep in Old Age

Sleep
is a tossing trip

As if repenting, as if adulating,
two hands on the chest
in a most lowly posture, curled posture....

Lowlier and lowlier
suspending myself here and there
naked body naked heart drifting
to find the me I've shed turning a baggage in tow;

a trip taken weary, to not tire out,
could I reach quiescence which is naught
I hope it'll take me to a dreamless place where I clean forget
　　myself
lest the shadow of relations flit by my shoulder
Don't they call it waking from sleep
as one, drifting along the river of consciousness, not death
　　but like death
visits briefly then comes back

Retaining waves of breath, then attaining total quiescence
one would face numerous worlds
closing, then opening,
before falling asleep
Deftly turning sideway along the town of dreams

I hope to wake up from sleep
leaving alone, reaching alone

to wake alone,
sleep in old age

# Fire

Samcheongdong, an uphill road,
why do I see a fire
in a tree that has lost all the leaves and stands all bones
Why does a fire pass over a tree branch
that has lost all the green blood and faded into aged brown
Letters in the signboards lining on uphill pass,
I want to read them as a single word Life;
why is a fire burning
in the letter Life

Past the flour dumpling restaurant,
past the second-best sweet bean porridge restaurant,
foreigners now walking all together
I hope they will read the word Life as Samcheongdong,
as the Republic of Korea
The uphill road of Samcheongdong is the road to reading
    Art
One walks up and up again,
craves to walk up yet again, the road of Samcheongdong,
why is the fire blazing up

Why?
is it that the ten blue fires at my fingertips do not go out
as I push open my baby-toe-sized gate
bolted and turned into darkness all night long,
and at the crack of dawn walk up the road of
    Samcheongdong

# It Is No Mere Chance

It is no mere chance that I came to Bukchon

Nor is this hanok the size of a button on old man's silk
chogori*

I turn around

again turn around
slowly so slowly walking Bukchon turn around
to see my own life I've treaded

A small town Geochang lapped in mountains,
where now and then the sky opened and I missed Seoul
The fact that I learned the word Mother, the word Friend,
the word Love
Thus from mountains to Busan to the sea of Busan then to
Hangang, Seoul
How could it be mere chance
Sweet is everything in hindsight

I don't think I will ever go back again,
not ever,
but now I
turn around once more
and touch the bygone times

Touching,
look on sourly

the stairway of old age

---

*Chogori is a Korean jacket.

# Rain Sound Blossoming beneath the Eaves of Hanok

Rain sound falling on the tile-roof
beats like drumbeat,
the sound like flowers flows down from beneath the eaves
The rain falling on the single span courtyard flows into me
to conjure up times past
Such musical instrument we had in my childhood too
The sound of rain pitapatted
When at thirteen I was sleepless
and hungry after a good dinner
and felt like someone's calling and calling over the fence

when the rain fell
pitter-patter drip-drop sprinkling pelting
a coxcomb by the jangdokdae* tittered
that it knew my feelings

Whispers of flowers blossoming under the eaves today
Putting down the book I was reading
I blossom to musical notes along with the rain all day

---

*Jangdokdae is an outside space, commonly a terrace, used
 to store or ferment food.

# Newspaper

Early morning
in the courtyard just the size of the white collar of my high
    school uniform
I pick up a bundle of heart-stirring news
It's warm

Thump! the sound falling in the courtyard
pulling the world's collar is the sound waking me
Opening a page then again turning over another
I speak my mind with world
And say bitterly that such is too deep a relationship,
or exclaim Ahh! moved, or feel a bit of tightness on one side
    of my back,
or want to pay subscription fee promptly
on seeing a poignant poem tucked in a corner

Thump! the sound of newspaper falling in the courtyard
The sound of world coming to me
The sound of world questioning me....

What am I to do today?

## Midair Buddha

Ahnguksonwon on Gawhoedong gil,

Buddha's birthday already past

they took down lotus lamps

Lights turned off

Buddha stands just the same

Buddha in the shape of midair

all of his body melded

into midair

to be near at hand

the crippled as well as homeless drunk;

to bump into each time they toss about,

Midair Buddha

# My Chairs

Back from a ten-day trip
the moment I open the door of my house in stillness
I see my chairs
weary of endless waiting
The chair in front of desk The chair in front of table The
    chair in front of dresser
Looking as though melting down to a pulp
were my chairs listening for my footsteps
with both arms open, all ears from head to foot for ten days
Three days, four days, still no me,
I suppose they stood with all their senses laid bare

Those…. the peace like God's lap
I suppose I leaned on as my family
For you
to stand is no punishment
The thing that as a cushion receives my body

that makes him a chair as only I sit there
For ten days the chair was famishing

## I Too Dry Up

If I too throw myself down
on the courtyard of next door hanok
where they spread out red peppers
will the sorrow oozing out of my body dry up

Do so
Like a pepper on the cusp of death by burning, holding dry
    seeds
totally sapless
as empty breasts,
like an anchovy dried out
though it took the sea into itself

thus with no thought....

# Music Comes Down

It's raining in Gyedong
It's raining in Gyedong

It's raining on the frightened backbone of a country with
    water shortage
When with restricted water supply, I hear, one savors a drop
    of water in the mouth

it's raining

Rain rising fast then swept like tidal waves on the arched tile-
    roof
The night when I look on the rain and listen, I flutter,
how can these be strictly rain sounds

Late night, that tune said to have made a young Korean man
    a Chopin
Soul's silence also rumbling, thundering
Light into a cascade
into a cascade of notes
that grand tune overflowing
mightier than Niagara, Iguazu Fall, that deafened us
Cho Seong-jin's Piano Concerto No.1
floods my room
Now it deafens me in rapture
This night's rain sounds
quite like that young man's fingers
giving the recital….

The welcome rain endlessly pouring down, promising more
    if wanted

## Bird Song beneath the Eaves of Hanok

I wonder who's turning on the light
Sunlight sings an aubade through hanji-lined window
A bird flushing from the eaves then pecking at the window
leads the chorus saying she goes first; sunlight saying he does
    leads the chorus again;
bright sun and bird dance in my room a sparrow's eye-sized;
as I open the window
sun passes through the 'flower card'-sized garden, fills a
    room just the size of a bird's footprint

Somehow that bird is mysterious
Is the bird's word a song, an urgent request, even asking for
    a handclasp
The sparrow's word endlessly rocks the morning
Calls me in full throat
I wanted to ask Who is this

# Wooden Veranda Floor

Dear me
who ever saw a wooden veranda floor the size of a puppy's
    tongue
When the sun plays on the wooden veranda floor the size of
    my ear
my foot soles are benumbed
Having crossed a thousand rivers
do I still have in my body
young foot soles wiggling
A thirteen-year-old
who sat on the floor of her old home, secretly yearning for
    Seoul,
her heart of hearts
quivers on this young veranda floor
I look at the young sky, sitting on the miniscule floor,
an attachment onto the house
as a body attached onto my body,
tickling
cradling sunlight

## Sweeping the Front of Gate

I sweep the front of gate just the size of a chestnut

Someone's thrown away a cigarette butt,
trees have dropped off leaves
and petals let faded flowers down
Clean swept are sighs of the one who passed by the front of
    my house last night,
tracks of those who shook off empty pockets then walked
    away,
lovers' unwillingness when at last unclasping each other

Summer is now smaller than a cabbage root

Sweeping the front of gate
nudging early autumn morning's cool vigor
I recall how in my childhood my father swept the courtyard
Father's hunched back more forlorn than autumn
· Inside it
are his cries
tumbling as leaves that have fallen

Like solitary meal of my father
who swept away all of his life as he swept his sorrows
autumn has come to the front of gate

# Artificial Tears

You use artificial tears, don't you

I've seen life's inundating tidal waves
overthrowing you a number of times,
it's a pity you should be using artificial tears
pressing down your body's pain spots of dry spell

You tell me to try a drop
Tears are a contagious disease
Seems to be a relief item now

Surging and rolling
those bloody sickening things,
those sloppy things, where have they all gone

Life's interior where a human vacates his place
to reflect the root of sickness without tears
and a hobbling animal is glimpsed
No way I can turn my eyes out heedless
to apply artificial tears

altogether I
leave artificial tears behind,
and as though transfusing tears
essay to hasten my steps
to that faraway forest of memory
where deep green cascades down

## Back from Geochang

I write Geochang and read it Mom
The land of Geochang I tread is mom's bosom
Back from Geochang I'm in my mom's bosom about three
   days
Whence it comes, the verdant foliage may have met her and
   come back
She may have wrapped a couple of rice cookies to hand over
   on seeing me
Attracting my eye, that one leaf lucid and green as can be,
like Chinese fringe tree, cooked white rice, worthy of May
   sunlight
I with teary smile meet the leaves

Back from Geochang I hum about three days
That Wonseodong is like Daedongri of Geochang;
no, no, that Gyedong is like Geochang;
not that
but that Gawhoedong is like Geochang;
that everything good is like Geochang;
no, that Bukchon is Geochang;
about three days
no, three months and ten days I
happen to liken all beauties to Geochang
And completely believe
here is my mom
So utterly believe

# Mount Deokyu, Mount Mother

I gaze at Mount Deokyu from Samchoeng Park

Have you been to Mount Deokyu
Ever been to Mount Deokyu sung in the Geochang
    Elementary and Middle School songs
The ridges in distant view captivating
yet so restful that one wants to forget everything and be
    cradled
Have you been to Mount Deokyu so liberal, apparently
    capacious, motherlike as they say, and one just breathes
    out Mother
That ridge liberal and capacious,
I brought forth all
Odd-shaped rocks and inaccessible precipices of Mount
    Deokyu leading
Muju and Jangsu, Geochang and Hamyang; Gucheondong
    Valley and Hyangjeok Peak;
that grand Baekdudaegan Mountain Range;
I brought forth all

Do you also know the wise Mount Samshin, Mount Jiri; I
    brought forth all
Mother Mountain whose spirit throbs
whose every steep mountain pass is so filled with high spirits
that the sacred empyrean over Cheonwangbong, Banyabong,
    Nogodan, offers hand

What Mount Deokyu says
is what Mother says

Samcheong Park deigns to tell me

## MERS*

Gyedong's alleys are all deserted
Gawhoedong's alleys are all deserted
Wonseodong's alleys are all deserted
Bored Changdeok Palace, Samcheongdong's winds in pines
prowling, waving;
the radio says
another died and three more are quarantined
and five more confirmed

In the deserted streets of Bukchon
floats about anxiety
and round the national flag flutter sighs worried for monthly
    rent payment

An afternoon one sorely misses
footsteps of people that breathe and move
I wonder what glasses would do
on the twin eyes that see the country too small

MERS takes people away
sets people apart
brings fear of people;

such alienation,
shunning people
turning backs to people,

the worst of human punishments

---

*The name MERS is an initialism for Middle East
    Respiratory Syndrome.

# Spring on the Way

Twenty below
I set myself on the tallest tree
The moment the branch bends,
the giddy moment I clutch the branch with all my might
I say there's nothing on earth but one tree branch
The body the closest to my life
My body already moved to a branch
Life stiffened thinner than a branch

For a split second I was no more on earth

When the will to fasten the whole body to the branch
        becomes a flame
to blaze up in ice wind
and at last one life trembles, shrinks breathless,
the instant bitter wind is ready to obliterate to the last leaf
the instant the branch bearing my body is ready to snap off

what's the most touching language on earth
what's the word one must say even if they cut off his tongue?

What do you think it is?

For winter semester
we have the last day of class today

# A Room to Myself

The window is now loose
It has talked that much with me

Korean paper lining the room door is in tatter
My monologue has been too lengthy

The wallpaper has ugly spots
I've had frequent sniveling

Why is darkness in this room
so tough,
I can't jab it with my fingernail

The glow watch's minute hand, flashing blue,
a fruit knife length, aimed at me;
the glimmering tip of eaves
turns into a rapier
striking terror into me

This single room
smaller than a key hole,
a deadly weapon
aimed at me today

## Influenza

Late night in January when

you lose your footing and slip is a night when icy

wind, so unruly, maybe slapped on the cheek somewhere, is
    in a rage

A night when flesh and bone all over, even blood, throb in
    great pain,

every door shut, the heart shut

A night when someone with a new hoe willfully tears my
    whole body to pieces

Still not enough, forcing its way, rattling,

keen wind from artic Siberia I breast;

the letter 'lone' in loneliness bolts up

to unsheathe a rapier scintillating sharp to cut the wind
    asunder

## Autumn in Bukchon

A corner of tile of hanok
taking on the color of coxcomb soars up
The eaves of this house
and the eaves of that one
are having a lovers' quarrel
like roosters butting their combs

An afternoon in fall
replete sunshine raining down,
in the backyard of hanok too
warm sunshine lazes away

# One Word

Like a radish gotten pulpy
all hollow inside

riddled all over
blighted

even in a storm
muted like this

there's one Word strictly given
for one day

Even in a strip of noodle
all mushy and going down the drain

there's a Word that holds the sun rising, the sun setting

# A Chest Called Kindness

I will make a chest named Kindness
Make a chest
anyone will snugly put his heart in
Of woods, camellia, I want to make it so soft
that it will last thousands of years

I will make a chest named Sensibility
Make a chest
anyone will trust and want to talk quite frank
Of woods, zelkova, I want to make it solid
to hold joy, anger, sorrow and pleasure

When Kindness and Sensibility marry
and give birth to Allgentle and Allheart
and raise them gently and sensibly
then those who keep punching, knocking, to their hurt,
smart no more at the laughs
from Allgentle and Allheart's home;
in a little alley in Bukchon yonder is suchlike home

# Rumpled

The morning sun rises

Will it smooth out?

The western sky, alight, flames up

Will it smooth out?

The shoulder line that has never once been straightened out

is rumpled up

This rumple

not to be smoothed out

if not by the heart whose ice has turned fire

Crouching down

before the hanok the size of my maternal grandmother's
    half-worn silver ring,

me

## Before Patchwork Wrapping-Cloth

Is this all the light or shade of the world

One's country, old home, memory, aching heart
so stitched together
in just same size and length; it's like seeing a mouth shut in
    silence

As to my life, how can it be of the same size and length as
    that
For a banner in some alley, I think, the entire Korean
    Peninsula is not enough
and while there's an area where one can be free-spoken,
a banner in some alley
whose slight wave benumbs the whole body
I'll be forced to not open my mouth but keep quiet

How can it be same as that
In some alley of life
there's a void where I could not ever open my mouth but
    stand mute
and some small vein, after a series of ruptures, plainly shows
    stitches

In hindsight, like a world map,
vastly stretching and whose ends I don't know
with some parts clearly visible to the eye

ragged
patchwork of my life
I see before a small patchwork wrapping-cloth hanging in
    Bukchon's shopping center

## Fresh Green on Cue!

On cue!!
Somebody must have shouted out Begin
Impossible to tell from where to where, my part from your
    part,
fresh green spreads out the world over
Couldn't stop it
Fresh green's stage spreads out, green here, green there,
    everywhere
Can't stop it
On the edge of fresh green's stage is me Existing on the
    same stage,
this life green as green can be
This stage where the dead can never stand together
Let us not be sullen and look doleful

## A Poet's House

In front of Gyedong Church

rising
like a canine tooth
like a bamboo baby hat

that house, there
a carrier delivers
a number of literary magazines then leaves

That house,
a poet lives there?

Invisible, but
ask if a new-sprung pole of this generation's literature
happens to be there inside the gate of that house

# Part II

## Samcheong Park

The day rain falls soft
I walk up Samcheong Park, with an umbrella open like the
    heart
Bukchon is bathed just right
so the road up to the park
feels light as though a long conflict has come to
    reconciliation

Such radiance amid misty rains
May's verdure is so deep that the green sunlight
shines upon the warps of my mind even

Heaven seems to prepare different sunlight each season

The rain, as it is, is like a pretty child next door
and the green sunlight like a kind letter expected tomorrow;
the Samcheong Park
where I walk, holding an open umbrella like best friend
Once in a while in a life's page there's a day like this,
so the green sunlight radiant like this on a rainy day

## Bukchon Village Inquiry Office

Ready to see Bukchon?
Come
They show you capillary vessels of the Republic of Korea's
heart
Come
In ardent pink even in winter they tell you how to enter
Bukchon

You with sore legs, please take a rest
It'll let you take a pleasant first step into Bukchon's
heartthrob
When it's cloudy, or rainy, or the sun bursts out bright,
enter into the midst of Bukchon's pines
Autumn winter spring summer
dear visitors are always under hanok's wings

Look, feel, exchange smiles,
then hanok village will beam with smiles

Look
On a strain of the evening sun setting
lightly, slowly
with a wavery gaze
with a keen eye, look

You scan with your two feet, with your heart,
you'll see a history written in fine-wrought workmanship
and paintings by artists who painted to the last drop of their
blood
and place after place, love of country at the cost of life

Regrettable if not seen, heart-aching once seen,
yet you cannot fail to catch the singular word Beauty,
Bukchon

Come
They show you in pristine color like a bud even in autumn

## Yushim Temple Site

Sleepless night
In the gray dawn, at times with no sign of people,
as I push the gate open and step out, right there
the Yushim Temple site
The historical house that was the reception room for
    patriots
In front of the gate, now turned into a guest house,
I call Manhae Han Yong-Un,
stroke the bulletin on the gate, telling his primary role in 3·1
    Movement,
stroke again the letter "Yushim" signifying that at this site
    the magazine Yushim was launched,
then essay to call a few times, Sir!
Is a monk not a man
Or rather, is he not the poet who wrote Silence of Lover
Tying traditional white coat's string, he opens the gate
Hands ink-stained, a brush in one hand,
eyes overly sunken, his is a sleepless-ten-days-or-so
    countenance
I say Let's drop it all and enjoy the cool air;
he says Let's drop it all and go out
He didn't even ask what is this woman
no, not even look at my face
but we drop by the night duty room of Choongang High
    School in Gyedong, walk the playground;
Baekdam Temple is far from here? I ask,
he just looks calmly in that direction,
then shoulder to shoulder we were coming down an alley in
    Gyedong

46

What a bliss this is
I got pretty plucky
daring to go as far as holding his hand, looked sideways,
and none but a wind, calling for spring, was wafting into my
    armpits

## Face of Bukchon

Is there anyone eager to know his own face
even while looking into the mirror
If you're eager to know your true face
then try to walk Bukchon regardless of season

Over there somebody walking
Those women in hijab
Over there an English couple, their eyes wide open,
looking for something
Chinese Families having street food and happy going Wa Wa

Take a good close look,
it's none other than your own face

A wagtail's wingbeat circling round as if oblivious of hunger
    a moment
enchanted by the space fairer than scenery
amidst sky and mountain and hanoks,
or by the underside of eaves of hanok,
it's all your face as well

When your heart breaks and
you ache, or something, come to Bukchon and walk
There you shall see
another face walking up in great stride

Your self-portrait
possibly drawn by Jeongseon Jang Seungup,* Cheongjeon
    Lee Sangbum*

When you walk and see Bukchon
surely you shall meet your own face

---

*Jeongseon Jang Seungup (1843-1897), pseudonym Ohwon,
    was an artist during the latter part of the Chosun
    Dynasty.
*Lee Sangbum (1897-1972), pseudonym Cheongjeon, was
    an Oriental painter who cultivated original landscape
    painting.

## One Hundred Years, Gyedong

Gyedong begins with alleys
Savory seasoning called alley makes Bukchon what it is,
this and that alley are all historical sites
Any alley friendly and not to miss out
In that alley is history's big, bright eyes
In 1914
the name Gyedong was registered
In Gyedong
past the washing ground
where Gyedong's women washed in the water from the
    palace where the king washed his face
then again
elapsed the era of Japanese imperialism,
afterwards, the Korean War, the Industrialization era with
    New Community Movement
and then came the AlphaGo era

By the main road at Changdeokgung 1-gil
is the home site of Mongyang Lyuhwoonhyung
Next to it, Bohun Building is where after the 1945
    Emancipation
the Chosun Preparatory Committee for Founding the
    Nation was established
Again
Chungang High School at 1 Gyedong,
there too, meetings for defending the nation were intense
The 1919 3·1 Movement was ignited in the night duty room
    of Chungang High School
So too, was neighboring Yushim site; breathless was
Gyedong defending the nation

Now a paradise of cafes,
but those who tread Gyedong know that its blood is still hot
That it still lights up when chafed

Are Gyedong's one hundred years
not Korea's blue blood and red history?

## Ahnguk Station

In Suseo Station where I lived was the homecoming, my
    steps in weary fatigue,
and Mount Daemo's trailing skirt swirling in chilly wind
    round about my neck
Over ten years I frequented the place
In my life's station, Suseo Station got further away
and my eyes follow Ahnguk Station nearly everyday
Winter evening when I return at ease
from Ahnguk Station to Ahnguk Station
to open with chilled hand a gate like a cosmos petal
there awaits in the yard like twin cosmos petals
a familiar visitor named 10-degrees-below-zero
Three layers of comforters in shivery cold hanok room,
browsing through literary magazines at three a.m., once
    opening the window to see;
I ask myself if this is Ahnguk Station here
A night when my melancholy puts on a wool cap
and demands for gloves as well;
when the illnesses accompanying my body, grown old and
    spent, hobble;
the hour when arboreal wind in Changdeok Palace and
    sylvan wind in Samcheong Park
pass before my house and head for Gyungbok Palace, hand
    in hand;
I wonder if my life's Ahnguk Station is as yet doing well

# Hibiscus of Gyedong

Two hibiscus trees in full bloom in Gyedong Church's front
    yard
The purple and white are abloom, softly calling the Republic
    of Korea

When you open the door, hibiscus bursting fuller and
    greeting
White hibiscus is a man, purple a woman,
and the two trees a couple, I think

The couple do not laugh out loud
are not dolts that can't even speak out
say hello to every passer-by
blithely sway to the flow of church hymns

have high spirits, have humility
unbroken in a storm for all its beating
quietly illuminate alleys of Gyedong;
a mother walking with a child in her arms
and teaching the child hibiscus, I perceive, is the schoolroom
    of Gyedong

How very seemly when the couple each lays down blossoms,
rolling up petals and letting fall in drops;
believing when fallen hibiscus is gathered and petals gingerly
    unfolded
therein is written the will of the Republic of Korea to live
    today
and the challenge of the Republic of Korea to live tomorrow,

conveying to each other only in their final fall their
    unspeakable hearts;
hibiscus couple in an alley of Gyedong

# Hanok

Is hanok the mother of Bukchon
Is Bukchon a child of hanok

A hanok, anyway, is a person whose heart you can hear

Not one with a beating heart only, brashly spoiling the
    appearance,
but one with great personality
modest and knowing when to be regal
saying what he has to say and forbearing anger

Making a long arm—what midair is she pointing at—
so elegant is the figure of the arm
I want to bow politely under the eaves
Want to cherish the gracefulness near at hand

When I incline my ear close to the gracefulness
this person's sentiment also is so tender
unending is the love story with sunlight and soft wind
seeping through the hanji-lined window
seeping through wood fragrance

O grace warm and captivating
Hanok is a living person
A living love
Today, too, breathing deep, she takes in a person

## Gyedong Arirang

Arirang Arirang Arariyo, going over Arirang Hill
My lover going away from me gets sore feet in less than 10-
    li*

I hear the bathhouse will disappear, where you bathe
    stretching yourself,
something unimaginable in a small hanok
The bathhouse frequented for forty fifty years isn't just a
    bathhouse
It was a resort and a solace to live through a day
The shabby bathhouse, where old ladies washed each other's
    back, mutually uplifted spirit, was pretty poor friend
That the bathhouse, poor but melting the whole body, will
    be gone
is as sad and disheartening as losing hubby in death

They say the hardware store will disappear The pitiful-
    looking barber shop too will soon disappear
The drug store has disappeared, is gone
The uncertain dry cleaner's is something just to be thankful
    for;
will the development boom invading alleys of Gyedong
aided by Chinese tourism craze ever expand Korea, I
    wonder

Samcheongdong's bright verdure also peers with doubtful
    eyes,
tall trees in Changdeok Palace too are wont to ask one
    another how things are going
Gyedong is busy putting on new clothe

yet people coming and going, close-lipped, missing
    something.
say hello in the morning alley
Falling asleep uneasy, waking with misgivings,
saying Gyedong is not Seoul but Gyedong,
dense hanoks brushing shoulders and mutually depending;
Gyedong

Veggies her-re!!! Fruits her-re!!!
Morning trucks calling for people,
a place where rural sentiments are alive
Where is Gyedong going,
with its endearing winter night cry, Sweet-rice-cake
Everyday, from head to toe, people scenting changes,
Gyedong Arirang

---

*Li is a length of a half-kilometer.

## Dongrim Knotwork Shop

When you come today

I'd like us to spend a night at Rock Gojae*
Shall we stay up a night at Tranchae*
Pines will softly rustle in the court,
we will be thrilled as if we've traveled to five-hundred-years-
    ago

Isn't this genuine Korea within Korea,
trees of hanok filling tacit silence with fragrance
The floor will be boiling hot
and hanok's bedroom cozy and restful

How delightful to have a good breakfast
that goes well with hanok
then drink a cup of quince tea

When we go to Dongrim Knotwork Shop
you'll be all smile, so happy
Handcraft of Korea is the breath of Korea
A sweet smile of Korea

You'll see pendants belts pouches dangle-pieces hair-strings
stretched and bent and rolled in wisdom by Korean hands
whose endurance abides

This neighborhood keeps one's eyes busy
Korean talent recreating to suit modern times
You'll see our true Korean Korea
your heart astonished, your blood lit up

Gawhoe Folktale Museum, Bukchon Handcraft Experience
    Center, Han Sangsu Embroidery Museum, too,
you enter hesitantly then become happy, eyes shining

If you'd like to go see fairly modern times, then Folklore
    Museum
As we go to the tea house Memory Lane and have coffee
listening to 70s music
will we further open our hearts and grow friendly
will we want each other
In this world with limited time and no fun....

---

*Rock Gojae is a hanok hotel in Gyedong, Bukchon, whose
    large stone courtyard provides artistic atmosphere. It is
    also the founding site of the Diagnosis Association.
*Tranchae is 90 years old hanok guest house. Located on a
    hill, one can have a panoramic view of Bukchon from
    there.

## Gawhoedong Catholic Church 1

Is this a Catholic church here?
Raising a question
I enter the hanok where the leading hand halts,
there's the agonizing statue of Virgin Mary, Baby Jesus in
    her arms
Mount a flight of stairs next to it, or step right in,
in sight is the history of Gawhoedong Catholic Church

Thenceforth I will mount the stairs of joy
seeming like a midair-walking heart aloft
like the center of my life here
like the terminus for my soul in this place
or rather,
like my life's starting post anxious, giddy and tearful

57 Bukchonro, Chongrogu
Any plot of Bukchon is all hallowed ground
April the fifth, 1795
saw the Korean church's first dedication mass
The first mass by Priest Moonmo Joo, who first opened the
    heavens in the land of Chosun
rang from Bukchon, and Gangbuk, Jongro, the Han River,
    Gangnam,
rang out Chosun, the Republic of Korea, like the Holy Body
    lifted high;
having bravely weathered bloody winds of Eulmyo and
    Shinyu Persecutions
here stands the Gawhoedong Catholic Church
sanctified, silently bowing down;

even now
cries of blood of Choi ingil, Yoon Yuil, Joo Moonmo, Gang
    Wonsuk, martyred,
though sunk down, and down hundreds of years,
are clearly heard to hearkening ears;
the dynasty, which was the root of persecution, shoots forth
    buds of faith again;
Chosun's last
King Uichon Lee Kang and Queen Uichon Kim Sook are
    baptized at last as 'Bio' and 'Maria';
thus is proclaimed that the blood of martyrdom revived and
    triumphed


Who has guided such a history
At last all kneel, lift up both hands as one grain of faith;
here's the one
that embraces, soothes gaping wounds and bruises of long-
    winding history;
A place where love's blood courses, holding and clasping
the deformed, bent, twisted, hobbling, lop-sided, with
    misshapen mouth,
those ugly, ignorant, destitute, unable to find own mind,
though small as if eyes might hold
A land of miracles flowing with flowers of faith, with trees
    of history,
Gawhoedong Catholic Church


One man who's been hovering, wandering, seeking a desire
    again today, only to return weary
Gawhoedong Catholic Church
is bighearted still waiting for us with twain open arms

## Gawhoedong Catholic Church 2

Five in the morning
I push the front gate open to leave the alley
The hour darkness just shed black robe to change into new
    bluish one
The hour roadside pines hurriedly get up
and wind in Samcheong Park washes face early
and hanok village rubs eyes shaking off sleep
Two hands two feet two eyes two ears all join in one thought
I push open the Gawhoedong Catholic Church door and
    enter,
cross myself
in the bright blue light coming through the window

From creation to now, from now to creation,
through time's byway, travels vast light

My body disappeared, two hands folded in spirit,
and a brief moment past
there's a hand suddenly come in touch with my stretched
    hand
There's a joy springing, suffusing the whole body

Infinite is the gift of Mass even if you figure by involution

"I wish you peace"

Exactly from this point on the Mass grows fervent again

"Only just speak a word, I shall soon be well"

# White Pine of Gyedong*

Changdeok Girls' High School in bygone days
A time when in my student-teaching days I was first called
'Teacher'
Age twenty-one when life was overbrimming with splendor
Now it is the Constitutional Court, a weighty name

A White Pine I greet in my morning walk
and bow down then pass on my way home
That person, the only light of the Republic of Korea, not
losing the whiteness
although he looks on our country's history
A White Pine upon whose sight I end up bowing my head
somehow

Maybe that forked White Pine made the map of the Korean
Peninsula

Is this the mark of a white tiger; could be the train of a
scholar's traditional outercoat through 500 years

Why fork off into two,
making our hearts still more sore, the White Pine of the
Republic of Korea
Herein I see one root,
the white-clad folks' light joined in one
and the two branches meeting in one armful circle

---

*The tree is a 600 year-year old white pine within the
Constitutional Court, designated natural treasure no. 8.

# Rickshaw

I see a rickshaw carrying a young woman in mini skirt
run through Gawhoedong, through Samcheongdong
A young man in a golden yellow cap
is pulling the rickshaw
Carrying a Chinese couple
an English couple
rickshaws are running an alley of Gyedong

August 1, 2015
On a sweltering hot road as if the sun beat down on
    Bukchon only
one runs Samcheongdong alley
carrying a French couple both in Korean costume

Those rickshaw riders
are all Hwang Jinis

Hwang Jini getting out of a rickshaw, her head slightly atilt
Poetry! Love! Man! Power! Promises!
That woman whose face singly commanded the whole world

Look at that, a rickshaw!

In a heartbeat the rickshaw is drawn back to hundreds of
    years ago
In Bukchon there's neither past nor present

In the village of clustered hanoks
one breathes in the scent of Korea's inner flesh

The one in the rickshaw
and the one watching are all
going past an age

## Date in Korean Costume

A woman and a man, twenty years of age,
are strolling about in Korean costume
How very beautiful

Over there, no, here too,
a youthful lady shy of just twenty goes with her boyfriend in
    Korean costume
They have traditional men's hat and woman's winter hat
    each
Bukchon is like the warm courtyard of mother's old home

Shall I also stroll about in Korean costume
Shall I be a wife to a learned man and walk about,
even my heart back to one hundred years ago

Bukchon goes well with Korean costume
When youths in Korean costume stroll abreast
Gawhoedong Gyedong Samcheongdong
Bukchon is in spring, flowering throughout four seasons

Winter jasmine, forsythia, azalea, burst forth in blossom,
Japanese apricot tree and magnolia worthily take pride in
    their figures,
cherry flowers make Bukchon dream gloriously,
crape myrtle and cockscomb smile brightly
Bukchon with cosmos waving, nodding in cool breeze

Youths in Korean costume walking the streets, Bukchon
    springs to life
into a nature's garden

Young man and woman in Korean costume kiss on the
        street
Burst into crisp laughter
Hand in hand,
I guess they'll brightly go on an outing to an ancient palace
Korean costume
is another pattern of love

## Baek In-jae's House*

In 1913, during the Forced Occupation Period by Imperial
    Japan
they built a hanok with black pine wood from the Yalu River
and that, with the cutting-edge two-story main building;
what a magnificent curve of hanok

Japanese-style hallway and floor are sharply contemporary
yet it was lucky that they could build here a hanok like this
Besides a tall gate
the front yard large yet cozy,
the elegance of the main house ahead of time,
the garden fixed in curve is very pretty
A hanok standing over a century
amid the crash of spear and sword during the Japanese
    Colonization Period so insensible,
Baek In-je's house still beautiful
I see the tile eaves resembling two hands stretched upward
have kept self-respect and honor unyielding to the winds of
    time
I don't know why I'm so moved to tears
to see how Chinese and European tourists pour in
and take pictures
Shaking out bits and pieces of the time lived out in the name
    of hanok,
a winter afternoon in Bukchon

*Built in 1913 by Han Sang-ryong, the CEO of the Hanseung Bank, the house ownership passed to Choi Seon-ik of the same bank, then in 1944 to Baek In-jae of Seoul, the leading figure in medical world then. The house was designated the cultural treasure no. 22 for its architectural, historical value, and then open to the public as of November 2015.

## Jeongdok Public Library

A place where the young blood of Gyunggi High School
  boiled
A place located right at the end of the pit of Bukchon's
  stomach
A place where those who come and go drop by at least once
to listen to Bukchon breathing
Where one meets spirit of the book
Where sin and evil surreptitiously rummage a book
Where the mind expands in scintillating light
and the buds of art burgeon here and there
and one unable to find a way by himself forges a way of the
  mind
Where even on a cloudy day one grasps a blue ray of the sky
  and draws to himself
A place where a wisteria, under which folks sit,
chillingly entwine ever more
screening the sky, giving people rest
Who knows if wisterias underwent some war among them,
  not a drop of blood shed,
if they so woefully ended up joining their bodies, saying I
  can't live without you,
even so
quit shallow human translation utterly
The wisteria, solely to let people rest,
lights gingerly her blue blossom lamp to shine on their
  minds,
tells them Rest, Rest even a moment

Jeongdok Public Library
where one takes away a full gain, body and mind at rest

# Seokjeong Boreum Well Site*

Step into the alley of Gyeddong,
pass Manhae House and Kim Seungsu Memorial Hall,
climb toward Jungang High School,
then stand before Seokjeong Boreum Well site
that makes you listen intently

Giving clear mind as you stand still,
even now Father Joo Moonmo of 1794
would likely sprinkle holy water on your forehead
and Father Kim Daegeon readily appear to give benediction,
this Boreum Well Site,
the mere shape yet preserved,
is where the holy water's power to wake the soul is intensely
     palpable

This well Father Joo Moonmo used for holy water in the
     first Mass in the land of Chosun,
we hear, granted somebody's hope for a son
and in the persecution of Catholic Church became bitter so
     folks couldn't drink of it;
no wonder there were those who knelt before the wonder-
     working well

When my heart is unsettled
I wash it in front of the Boreum Well
in good earnest as in receiving holy water from Fathers Joo
     Moonmo and Kim Daegeon

The taste of that well-water unmarred even after hundreds
     of years
Today, stroking the design of true love in front of that site

I moisten my tight throat
My knees resound with ardor

No water, but the heart of fire remains
to get itchy
the scars of my faith so hard to flame up as it is;

history rolls on
and foreigners pour in
nonetheless the Seukjeong Boreum Well site whose honor
    is preserved in that solitary lot

---

*This is the well Fathers Joo Moonmo and Kim Daegeon
    used for the country's first holy water. The water was
    clear for a fortnight, turbid for the next; hence the name
    Boreum (fortnight) Well Site.

# That Man, Jeong Saegwon*

Hanok Village
31
Gawhoedong, Jongrogu, Seoul

Gazing up at the roof
I take a notice of a plate of ark shells
neatly arranged

Such, I marvel, is
the beauty of ancient Chosun

Affection prudence
acuity abounds properly

Nimble and dexterous
are lines of the eaves slightly reared
like the shape of the toe of traditional sock
Seems to me it might take wing
or an elegant woman in Korean dress step out

By the way
a man called Jeong Saegwon
in traditional white coat is stepping out
The man who gave all his asset to create in Bukchon a hanok
	village by himself
The will to plant Korea in the midst of Japan
even under the torture and serving his term of imprisonment
is in every way hanok village

He is gone but
here

the universal curve, love of country, and will
of the Republic of Korea
breathe alive, within reach, to be desired

Jeong Saegwon, that man,
the Republic of Korea must earnestly clasp his hands once

In his will to leave behind not swords and guns
but traditional culture at any cost,
the single-mindedness touching the sky
in the spirit of Korea, white outer coat flapping,
to that patriotism
we must bow low once

---

*He is the constructor who built the large-scale hanok
residences in Bukchon in 1930s. Providing half of the
Product Promotion Campaign budget, he orchestrated
Self-Support Movement, and assisted Independence
Movement through Singanhoe. For contributing
Korean Language Society building, he was tortured, all
of his property forfeited.

# Woodland Library

Enter Samcheong Park, right there is the library
Inside and out are all books
There are more books outside
Plentifully heaped up are
seasonal books of spring and summer and fall and winter

People read books in the library
then go out
to read a lengthy series of novels, looking on the groves
In a book of a child's-palm-sized new leaf
they read a children's poem;
in the fresh wind of Samcheong Park
letters sink deep in the blood

Why is a book in the woodland library more definite,
those famished in the mind taking a roundabout way in the
     world
are filled just with basic side dish
in the library in the wood
Look at the scenery
The side dish infuses the body with nature's nutrition we
     must know of,
pours down the throat the air we must drink each day

That woodland library,
a sumptuous table of organic foods for the mind is set there
     all day long everyday

## Changdeok Palace Stonewall Walkway

Sun's pace gets rather faster
When the sun's shadow slants to one side
I walk Changdeok Palace stonewall walkway

The hour I stub my toe against thin film of darkness
The hour the sky blazes up on one side

As temperature drops under the stonewall walkway
I walk by the stonewall, a huge patchwork wall,
and hear the leaves of Changdeok Palace deeper and quieter

Passing by Spatial Building*
past Woohyun Workshop
past Mago Café
and Tea Museum
then sound of darkness falling from beyond the wall

Without understanding I nod
In the alley of Wonseodong are voices of those who dwelled
    in the Palace
Their footprints too can be traced
There are their shouts too running down the marrow in
    silence
One would also hear in Changdeok Palace stonewall
a single cry the sky gives like red twilight-glow burning,
    flowing
As foot-chilling darkness gathers
one can hear a sorrow forced to swallow soft loneliness

Never once have I spoken of myself
but the small tile-roof atop the stone walkway ceaselessly

unfolds to me a life of hundreds of years ago
This stone walkway I am walking around for the umpteenth
time

Goh Heedong's Residence before my eyes awakes my whole
body*

Right before dragging out my itchy life
I hasten my step to my house where a paper lamp lights up

---

*Constructor Kim Soogeun's spatial building.
*The nation's first oil painter Goh Heedong lived in this
residence.

## Good Luck This Spring

From Mr. Sacheon I received: Good Luck This Spring;
    Many Blessings to Family
The finesse of his calligraphy is already famed
yet at this excessive gift I suddenly hear a voice saying Good
    luck
I told him I was in a rush, bolted up
and ran home, Chinese quince tea unfinished

The two having been affixed aslant on coxcomb-sized front
    gate
it feels like all Bukchon's luck is rushing over here
for hopes and prayers to come true
I don't know why I'm so satiated
with this calligraphy known to outdo a session of exorcism,
perhaps the spring of my life is now on the way

Commending to the eight words
a year's helpless wishes
I cast my eyes leisurely to budding trees

Might I read Good Luck This Spring as Good Luck Your
    Life
No one to open the gate
but I cry out loud once
Hello, there!
and open the gate wide and step in

# Bukchon Palace Villa

The house I live in, would it measure up to a couple of
    acorns
But
I have a palace for my villa
And I have a stately palace I resort to through time's byway
Hence that palace made of eco-friendly wood
everyone desires to own
A palace looking down on all of Bukchon and Jongro
What's more, it is a living, breathing palace
To give a hint, Samcheong Park itself is my palace
Who'd have a palace like this

People unknown to me freely haunt
my palace no rich man can easily own
I'd think it's because I am a magnanimous person
Trees woven and erected for the palace wall:
snowbell, spindle tree, tree of heaven, cherry tree, hackberry,
waving all over welcome me though I still don't know my
    palace name,
and care for my body in an eco-friendly way
When I go up at six a.m., already people are relaxing their
    bodies
Life is binding, so I guess they come to my palace to relax
    their bodies
I, being a magnanimous one, give away all my palace,

wave my arms a couple of times then come down
Spindleberry holds to me but I decline with "I'm aright"
and burrow under comforter in the room the size of a wild
    orange

## A Walk in the Alleys

Gyedong shines with alleys
Gyedong starting with an alley, round and round an alley,
then again leading to another
Past Hundae Building
past Bukchon Culture Center
round the house Manhae used to dwell in
round the house Kim Seungsoo used to dwell in*
round Ace Black-and-White Photoshop
then I walk by the tea house showing 60s' movies
I catch a glimpse of Audrey Hepburn passing by
In an alleyway with tiny little shops standing
I take a liking to a ware and smile;
should I buy and sample roasted rice cake
should I try a Jeongae cookie Miss Jeongae bakes
should I buy a necklace with the shape of a Korean sock
A walk in the alleys round an alleyway, me full just looking,
then round and round an alley leading to another
When I've passed by the front of hanok Catholic Church in
      Gawhoedong
it's about time my soul had lunch
I cross myself, take prayer food,
turn back to return, the homeward way is truly blissful and
      buoyant

---

*His penname Inchon, Kim Seungsoo is the founder of the
*Donga Daily*.

# The Queen's Palace Walkway

Should you cross the intersection leading to Insadong
and for a moment you stagger at the floral breeze,
then turn around
Turn around
and pass Poongmoon Girls' High School, stroll the Queen's
    Palace Walkway
Walking by Gamrodang to the left, the Queen's Palace
    Walkway to the right,
even the heart staggering for a moment shall tread bright
    exotic road
What country is this here,
what ideal, imaginary, idle country's alley here,
sense of fulfilment bursting from tiptoes
knowing this is an alley of Seoul, Korea
and the Queen's Palace Walkway, a name so pretty at that

one can walk serenely now and again
Touching quietness, and then into still larger,
treading low the road of silence,
I happen to shout Wow!
The Queen's Palace Walkway where shops
I'd love to stroke thrust out their chins,
Come, love me
At end of the walk is the site of Chosun Language
    Association*
so I pause for a moment

I've just walked out an alley
but it feels like I've walked out a floral road,
a languid afternoon on the Bukchon Palace Walkway

---

*This used to be Korean Language Research Society founded in 1921 by the followers of Joo Shigyung (1878~1914) for the purpose of research and augmentation of Korean language.

# Eight Bukchon Classics

Just as a person has a heart, lungs and livers
Bukchon has eight classics
like those priceless organs

When you see Changdeok Palace over the stonewall
that's the beginning of Bukchon classic 1
When you walk up the stonewall walkway, at the deadend
you'll see tracks of palace people
Then you'll be standing at Bukchon classic 2

You turn around a bit, you see hanoks,
and Bukchonro 12gil opens up, it's Bukchon classic 3
When you see a family of hanoks, one embracing the other
    in good earnest,
all the way to Yee Joongu residence, it's Bukchon classic 4

When you come down Gawhoedong amid clustered hanok
    village
you're at Bukchon classic 5
Go up Bukchon at last, till Hanoks loom the largest of the
    world,
you're at Bukchon classic 6

You step in a quiet alley, your face spellbound by the hanok,
and feel affinity with Bukchon's people, that's classic 7;
step into the passage of stone stairs down onto
    Samcheongro,
you'll meet a solid rock sculpture, a great master
That's Bukchon classic 8

Eight Bukchon classics, like Seoul's breathing organs,
like the Republic of Korea's heart or lungs,
entirely controlling even one small vein,
are the very life of Seoul

## Flow, Flow, Blood!

You are the blood of Bukchon

When you walk up
and your friend walks up behind
Bukchon breathes long

If you've come to Bukchon today, you are the blood of
    Bukchon

Starting from Ahngook Station past the Constitution Court,
from Myungin Mask Museum
past Bukchon Museum where you get a whiff of art's old
    scent
then go up and up,
people coming and going are all
the blood of Bukchon

Those who plunge into indefinite appointments with friends
out of longing for Bukchon
and grab anyone on the street to ask the hanok's uphill and
    downhill
are all the blood of Bukchon
All the foreigners thronging
in their excitement about street foods,
having roasted rice cake, fried croquette and sushi on their
    feet
are also the blood of Bukchon

Those walking along Bukchon
fond of Bukchon, curious of Bukchon
The human intents

fully transmitting human blood into the heart of Seoul
is the very blood of Bukchon
Footsteps retracing from a wrong track are all
the blood of Bukchon as well
Today again Bukchon flows fast with red blood
Breathes in good health

# Sweet Revenge

My cap pulled over my eyes, a thick muffler around my neck,
I walk up Samcheong Park at dawn
up, and up,
then, with an Oh!, see vivid yellow flower buds in the snow
    lingering in cold wind

See a sweet revenge
said to generate alone body heat headbutting own body
to bloom before anyone else,
for other plants take all sunshine and insects as it's small and
    short

Lift up my head and admire the sweet revenge
said to rear the flower stalk before anyone else,
to rise against ice and lingering snow
with a sole intent: "Let me live out" "Let me flower"
and by all means gather sunshine in yellow
to get past existential threat,
which sounds like 21st century's theme

Fall to my knees to the sweet revenge
thawing with reserved body heat 20-below-zero chill
to rise with a prodigious smile;
it has another name
ice bird flower, for it blooms like a bird winging in the ice,
which I wish to be rather like

Want to bow down before the sweet revenge
—such a terrible name—
now in bloom tougher than a strong man,

yet its vivid yellow queen-flower with exquisite grace
astonishing a beholder

Why do I feel a knot in the pit of my stomach
when I see a sweet revenge?

# Holy Mother's Train

Early dawn
I open a magnolia petal of a door, draw a thread of darkness
In my hand is Holy Mother's train
What I drew is black darkness
and I've got a fold of sky-blue robe
I touch, I drink, I embrace
At once the hate and enmity reborn today dissolve away

The hate and enmity born at this dawn give an infantile cry
The knots of my mind and body also cry
In the afternoon even hate and enmity grow older
Before they grow any older, I make myself stop crying

The knots like tender shoots grow thick
each time I breathe, each time I speak
There flutter plumes of sin
popping out each time the muscle thickens

Each time, then, I draw the air
In my hand is Holy Mother's train

Late night
someone hung a green pine twig on my lipstick size door
I am going to do well all the while

Appears I will be reconciled before falling asleep

## No Crying

A root of my tears
I have planted in Samcheong Park
The rumor was that last summer's Samcheong Park was
    green
As green as it was, my whole body itched more than ever,
no shoots came out
and the ruins of my tears were arid

I've since had a couple of affairs I should cry my eyes out
    for,
and my crying perhaps lost, my inside sank down, cracked;
ay, ay, only horror remained, and not so much moisture in
    my sobbing
Winds staggering, unable to gain footing, faded into that
    silence
and occasionally rustled

Maybe my cries in a single file are rushing pell-mell to
    somewhere,
the lone heart with no way to take the lid off,
holding nothing but color of red blood, trembles
in a hand-chilling winter night's silence

Popping in a white sleeping pill
then waiting for complete sleep
I attempted at following muted cry
but how far can one cry follow another
Is it that the colder the age, only within cries one,
having tossed a question halfheartedly
lying in a dark room the size of a teardrop

I spend the night only just chasing away razor-sharp wind
that claws to cut me through the window hanji-lined in
    poke-holes

## Wedding Anniversary

Lush foliage shuddering and shuddering,
bawls as if breathing its last

I've decided to fasten a leaf on me Decided to fasten a leaf
    dripping
thick green, so much so that my ankles slip into it
Today, the wedding anniversary without you
Remember the young bride when the world shudders like
    this with lush foliage?
On the wedding anniversary you and I both in fact forgot, I
    fasten a leaf on me
Where have all those fresh leaves of a bride fallen off, since
    when
the pristine field has become bleak, far too long I haven't
    felt your touch
No more agricultural insecticide but organic farming,
a motto I've heard much, but
worn with a world too vile, contrary to pure environment,
my life once sleek now has no soundness Terribly injured
Wherever that may be,
shall I pull up my comforter and text you Delivered or not,
    I "text"
and it's as though dark green leaves in the mountain facing
    my house are dashing in my direction as if upon some
    word
Scorching heat wave alarm is being texted
Marriage was something like a scorching heat wave warning
Wedding anniversary without you
Summer, green leaves fading farther and farther away from
    my body
Summer is going away

# Pooh

Oh my, it must hurt
As I've fallen on a rock and got my shin skinned,
her lips on my bloodied wound
and blowing poooh, poook....
the warm breath of my grandmother on mother's side
soothing away half the smart
When I whimper for all that, my grandmother would
apply saliva on her wrinkled finger
and say Here you go, blowing again poooh,
then the smart vanished clean away
and I played flapping my wings
Played flapping my wings like a butterfly
When locking eyes with a rose moss with bruised petals
I with lips like drops of water
blow poooh
rose mosses and touch-me-nots all at once burst out
    laughing Hohoho,
one summer noontime when mother's sorrows suddenly
    cease a moment

comes near me today
to blow on the heart's broken shin
poooh

## Vegetable Garden

After a little fall of rain, grasses grow much taller

Today I listen to moraengi grass' story, rising with her head
  held high

Grasses I pull out for uselessness have more to tell

My ears grow rapidly

Since I moved to Bukchon

shoe-repair man newspaper-delivery student sesame-oil
  businesswoman

hardware-store businesswoman old lady, 88, talking to me,
  I'm alive and kicking

Why so much to tell, the lowlier one is

Those standing outside the vegetable garden

Those on my mind, yet without a word

Poetry, I wait all day but you do not come, maybe close-
  mouthed today

I've come to the vegetable garden, unfold my manifold heart
  to hear the grasses' stories

and for the poem, take down a couple words from dictation,
  then fall silent once more

Maybe poets standing in a queue have taken all the stories
    of the lowly

# Postscript

## A Ladder Laid upon Time
## —written while strolling about Bukchon

Chang Seoknam (poet)

When it comes to a place, I am not likely to forget one to which I take a liking on a casual visit. It is not easy to like a person after one encounter, but regarding a place (this includes the time spent for meeting), after a single visit one can say "That's my favorite place". I may have a peculiar perception of space.

The place I for the first time in my life felt "Ah, so nice" is still vivid. Was I about three or four, four or five? A cold winter day, the wind hissing, there in the graveyard behind our house under the hill was no wind, nicely dried golden grass basking in the warm sun. And, except for the sound of wind passing distantly and occasional meadow bunting calling, it was quiet. I was at an innocent age with no knowledge that it was a burial site of skeletons, so the place and the time seemed to draw me, call me; upon my response, that place was the 'bosom' of infinitely tender quietness and sunlight and the high azure. I still cannot forget that hill's warmth on my back. In that bosom, smile was a spontaneous thing, and I remember I was sitting there languidly indulging in mild excitement as if playing some soft musical instrument. It may be that my memory of the place, a proper refuge from a discordant family, has been so reconstructed innocently.

As I grew up, that tiny place grew larger into an alleyway (that of Prague), into a building (Saemteo Inc.) or an entire village (Seungbukdong). Speaking of nature, when I met a great mountain valley (Hangyeryung in autumn), or a seaside vista (Hyupjae, Jaeju), I would experience the state of my mind transformed accordingly. This mindset led me, without a major conflict, to Seungbukdong, which I had once passed by feeling very good, and it's been already over twenty years since I planted the first tree here. In autumn I harvest over forty pounds of persimmons.

To go downtown from my house in Seungbukdong, there are roughly three different routes. The first lies in the direction of Hyewhodong, and the second runs through the tunnel in Samcheongdong. In general, these two routes are routinely taken. Because you can easily drive along these routes. The last route: you walk up the steep road called 'Bukjeonggil' behind my house, pass through the stone gate under the walls of Seoul to go over the rocky range down to Changgyung Palace, take a shortcut over the mountain behind Seunggyungwan down to Changdeok and Jongmyo, then go down to the Board of Audit & Inspection. When we kept a big dog I paid frequent visits to an arbor behind the city's enclosure. Night view of the east side of Seoul was spectacular.

I used to take this road to go downtown for business matters, deliberately giving myself extra time. I go past the byway between the Ministry of Unification building and the Board of Audit and Inspection, finally to reach where I can directly look down on Namsan. Steep though it was, I used to edge up the declivity beautifully, thanks to its proper breadth and ambience blunting one's sense of speed. This is the road that comes into what we call the upper Bukchon.

When I ascended this road, naturally a poem came to my mind. The poem's forte is its succinct evocation of the heart of the natural surroundings.

A fifteen-or-sixteen-year-old boy, an armload of peonies on the back of his bicycle, cries out in a voice like a pullet, "Flowers for sale!" going past an alley of old ink-black tile-roofed houses of the Yee dynasty. The voice pulses in the jade-green air best tinged in the world. From behind, a lady who wants some flowers opens a white paper-lined window, calls, "Flower boy, Flower boy, come this way," but not hearing this at all, the boy just keeps going, crying hard, "Flowers for sale! Flowers for sale!" When he has ascended the hill where there are no more ink-black tile-roofed houses, he quickly mounts the seat in front of the peonies and runs along, ringing the bells.
"A Great Day in Hanyang" by Midang, Seo Jeongjoo

In this poem's landscape, the appearance of the fifteen-or-sixteen-year-old flower boy is not a commercial one. We cannot but declare it the symbol of energy breathed into the village clustered with ink-black tile-roofed houses yet devoid of vitality (Bukchon was largely the residential area of the old doctrine powers toward the last of the Chosun Dynasty). A window opens, and a voice allures him, "Flower boy, flower boy, come this way," but he turns a deaf ear, and just goes on his way, self-absorbed. I picture a child who "has ascended the hill where there are no more ink-black tile-roofed houses, quickly mounts the seat in front of the peonies and runs along, ringing the bells." And try to figure the mindset that quickly mounts not the bicycle saddle but 'the seat in front of the peonies.' Perhaps this land's art and culture and 'grand tile-roofed houses continue unbroken, as we have an enrapture like this in a boy.

Word came to me that Mrs. Shin had a small tile-roofed house built one autumn in a corner of a place where this boy's bell ceases tinkling. Inwardly I was both surprised and glad. It may be because that was my own dream. I felt I could understand her mind well. And then, whenever I come to the vicinity, it has become a habit for me to stare about, wondering whereabouts of her house, or glance around with a hope to see her walk by haply. Did we ever come upon our acquaintances strangely so often in old villages.

I've heard rare stories that digging an ancient site in an ancient town may indeed bring a bonanza. This means therein lies a treasure hidden. It is simply true that in the strata of an ancient town are wholly preserved marks of time for us to take not for extravagance, but for food for life. Several scenes that I cannot but recall as I descend Gawhoedong road, Bukchon, ask me again what treasure lies in the time.

To begin with, as Mt. Inwang distantly comes into view I recall the *Inwang Color Map* by Gyeomjae Jeongseon, a beautiful secret story behind the painting coming to life as though it occurred only yesterday.

Mr. Choi Wansoo of Kansong Art Museum came to a very curious final interpretation…. He researched historical evidences that the great poet Lee Byeong-yeon, bosom friend of Jeongseon, died in the leap month May 29, 1751, when the latter was pitching into the project, and that the tile-roofed house shown on the right bottom is his own, which stood near the back wall of the Land Palace at the foot of Mt. Bugak. That said, it follows that the *Inwang Color Map* is the work the septuagenarian Jeongseon crafted with all his might for sake of his friend for six decades, then at the point of death. For it is a plausible translation that he, out of a sense of crisis that he may lose a lifelong friend, conveyed his solicitous heart praying for the friend's godsend recovery…. After some speculation, I confirmed in the *Diaries of the Royal Secretaria* the weather before and after the death of Lee Byung-yeon. That year, leap month May the 1st through the 18th it rained off and on, two to three days apart. And then for seven days from the 19th until the morning of the 25th a tedious rainy spell continued, and the long rain cleared up only in the afternoon of the same day. So then, it is certain that the *Inwang Color Map* was painted in the afternoon that day.... It also appears that Jeongseon strove to illustrate his old friend's virtuous and worthy character in Mt. Inwang's lofty spirit and in the immaculate line drawing of Lee Byung-yeon's house.

—*The Joy of Reading Ancient Paintings* by Oh Jooseok, from the section of *Inwang Color Map*

Unfortunately, although Mr. Oh Jooseok had gone to an early grave, his plainly researched account contributes to my steadfast attachment to this painting, and besides the painting, helps to grasp the gravity of the interpretation and annotation of it.

Another scene is the one involving the white pine seen over the fence of the Constitutional Court, and the housing site. It is known to be Yecnam Park Jiwon's Housing site. Apart from his immortal travel journey *Yeolha Diary*, one cannot imagine the history of our country's literature, however, I cannot but recollect the story of His Excellency Hwanjae Park Kyu-soo, his grandson, and his men's quarter.

The so-called idea of enlightenment was propagated, and the party formed, in the men's quarter at His Excellency Park Gyu-soo's home; one can imagine ever fresh how those young bloods, concerned for the country, resorted thither with bated breath. Realizing their country was dying; the youth not pursuing personal interests only; pressing on at the risk of one's own life.... Although the outcome was miserable, I feel I can see the shadows of the young as well as the many pioneers like Oh Gyungseok, Yu Daechi, flitting under that white pine, which stood in the heart of Bukchon.

There is yet another fragrant scene: a gathering called the White Tower School. The ten-story stone pagoda in Wongak Temple site was called the White Tower, as it was of granite; and there within the towering sight Park Jaega, Yee Seogu, Yu Deukgong, Yee Deokmu, and others, with Park Jiwon as their leader, gathered to haunt the place, and established the Positive School.

To visualize how they proceeded to compile an 'anthology' together is indescribably fragrant. It took place two hundred years ago already; but as one draws nearer to the White Tower (recalls the time presently bound and encased in glass), their spirit and poems come across as only of recent past.

It is like engaging in a happy reading to string together the scenes of past history imaginatively, if not precisely, each with hundreds of years' time difference, and fumble through them.

Years ago I went a few times to the Poets' Association office facing Changdeok Palace. It was about time when Mrs. Shin Dal-Ja was the president of the association. For one with my capability, it was a trip with no more to do than take a free meal. I was most likely imagining those things as I descended the aforementioned Bukchon road. Each time, it was a serious matter for me to look into the *dramatis personae* (there was none who was no poet!) Human nexus is an inexplicable thing, I learned that Mrs. Shin, at the close of her term with the association, had built her a small modest house entirely in Korean style in the outskirts of Bukchon, and moved in. Then the word came that she assiduously turned her excitement, as great as it was, into verse, before the fire die down. How consequential to set still anew modern landscape, modern delight, modern feeling on the basis of ancient topography, ancient delight, ancient sentences and poems. Whenever I see a small hanok again, I will perhaps remember this poem by her:

You do not need a large wall for putting up an address

You do not need a big garden for setting up one stick

Why need a large room for making up one's mind

While defrosting a bowl of frozen rice

a day the size of a grain of rice goes by

—"Coolness"

The time of our life is perhaps the size of a grain of rice. This, I believe, is the one poetry book that, by reflecting ancient history, reflects anew a poet's burden to love her own abode, to examine her time in life, and to sing the breath of life. This small remark I append to the big senior's poetry book. However, would it be an exaggeration if I say there's a sentiment like 'peony' in cherishing her poems?

## Gwak Hyowhan, poet

One autumn a couple of years ago, I went to the poet Shin Dal-Ja's housewarming party as she had moved newly into a ten-pyung-or-so hanok in Bukchon. Looking at the house name 'Gongildang, I could read her tranquil and full mind to empty out only to gather and fill up afresh, or rather, to reckon that emptying is filling. And today I open her poetry book *Bukchon*, and see it brimming over with small and large lives and everyday affairs thereof. The scenes created by the relics and persons encountered in alley after alley between Gyungbok and Changdeok Palaces, residents and visitors both, come flowing like flowers transformed into "rain sound blossoming beneath the eaves of hanok" that is Gongildang. Which is to say, Bukchon in "the most touching language on earth" becomes her mentor Mogwol, her father and mother, and Mt. Jiri nestling her old home.

I think I will go for a walk some sunny day, her poetry book, now "a pole of Bukchon", tucked under my arm. "Starting with an alley, round and round an alley / then again leading to another," I will go on past Seokjeong Boreum Well Site, walk up and down the home site of Mongyang, Yushim Temple Site, Gawhoedong hanok Catholic Church, then stop in at a shabby tea house to open a path for the mind. And will pore over that mind.

# About the Author

Shin Dal-Ja has published several poetry books including *Ardent Love, Paper*. For her elegant and gorgeous verse she was awarded the Gongcho Literary Award, the Jeong Jiyong Literary Award, and the Daesan Literary Award, among others. She served as the president of the Society of Korean Poets, and is a member of the National Academy of Arts.

## About the Translator

A recipient of numerous grants for her English translation of modern Korean literature, Cho Young-Shil has translated seven contemporary poetry books including *Paper* by Shin Dal-Ja (Codhill Press, 2018) and *Invisible Land of Love* by Chonggi Mah (Homa & Sekey Books, 2022).

www.ingramcontent.com/pod-product-compliance
Lightning Source LLC
Chambersburg PA
CBHW021342090426
42742CB00008B/709